# GRANDPA'S GARDEN

Written by Susan Swiat
Illustrated by QBN Studios

Copyright © 2023 by Susan Swiat
Illustrated by QBN Studios

All rights reserved. No part of this book may be reproduced in any form or by any electronic or mechanical means, including information storage and retrieval systems, without permission in writing from the publisher, except by reviewers, who may quote brief passages in a review.

For my grandson, B.J.  You continue to inspire me everyday! And to my husband for being the Grandpa that takes the time to plant the garden with the grandkids.

**One cold winter day when B.J. was small his Grandma made vegetable soup for them all.**

**But B.J. just wrinkled his nose and said, "Geez!"**

"I will NEVER eat vegetable soup… No, Siree!"
Grandpa just smiled and said, "Well…we'll see."

Later that year, just as spring did arrive, Grandpa prepared his garden outside.

He raked, and he tilled, and from down on his knees,
He said, "I could sure use some help if you please."

He gave B.J. a hoe and a packet of seeds
And showed him how to pull up the weeds.
They planted and covered, and watered them all
And marked each row with some string and a trowel.
B.J. asked Grandpa, "When will they grow for me?"
Grandpa just smiled and said, "Well... you'll see."

**So every day when B.J. would visit,
He would rush to the garden to see what was in it.**

**Day after day, he would check and then sigh, "There's nothing growing and I don't know why!"**

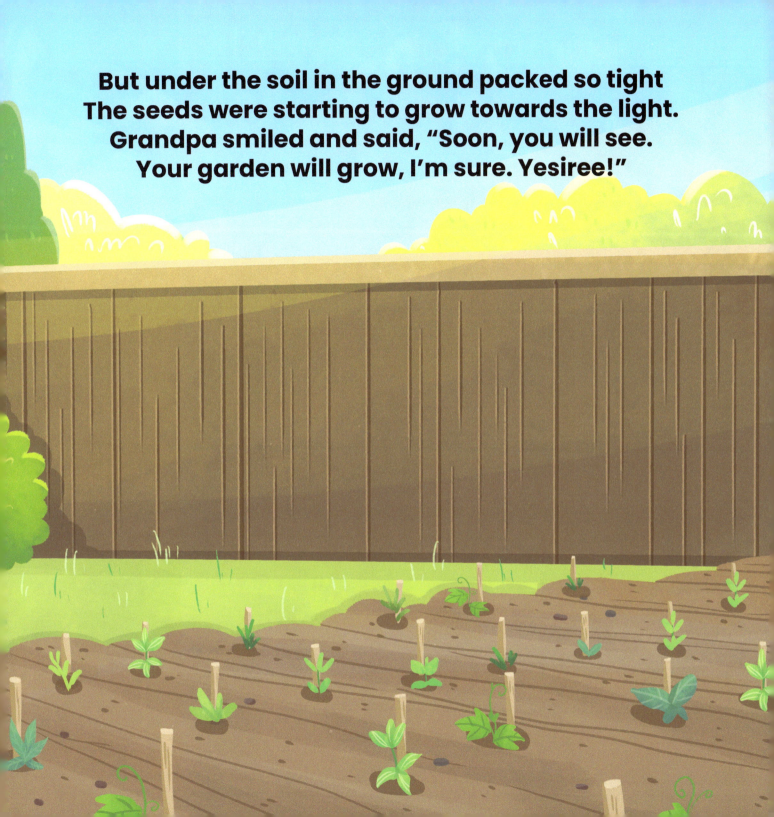

But under the soil in the ground packed so tight
The seeds were starting to grow towards the light.
Grandpa smiled and said, "Soon, you will see.
Your garden will grow, I'm sure. Yesiree!"

Then one glorious day, green sprouts popped through the soil.
And B.J.'s excitement could not be spoiled!
As the summer days passed, his crops grew and grew
The green tomatoes turned red
And he even tried a few.

A nibble here, and a nibble there and
B.J. started to become aware of
How yummy the veggies they were growing could be
The snap of a green bean, the crunch of a pea
The juice of a tomato eaten right off the vine
"These veggies," he thought, "actually taste just fine!"

As the days grew shorter, it came time to pick
All the veggies that grew. They had to work quick!
They harvested onions and garlic, carrots, and peas.
Tomatoes and green beans, and celery leaves.

B.J. was beaming with pride and was glad that his Grandpa had been there by his side! B.J. looked down at his basket so full and said, "Grandpa, what can we make with them all?"

Grandpa's eyes twinkled as he chuckled with glee,
"Vegetable soup sounds good B.J. Don't you agree?"
B.J. smiled and said, "I guess I'll try it and see!
Maybe vegetable soup will taste good to me!"

B.J. helped Grandma to chop, cut, and dice.
And into the pot went their veggies and spice.
Grandma stirred it up and let it all simmer.
"Want to try some soup now?" she asked as her eyes glimmered.

And as B.J. tasted the soup, his eyes grew wide with surprise.
He smiled and said, "Gee, Grandpa! You are so wise!"

"Especially when the vegetables were grown by ME!"

Printed in the USA
CPSIA information can be obtained
at www.ICGtesting.com
LVHW060728230624
783644LV00012B/43